HIV/AIDS
and employment

Date Due

BRODART, CO.   Cat. No. 23-233-003   Printed in U.S.A.

HIV/AIDS
and employment

Louis N'Daba and Jane Hodges-Aeberhard

International Labour Office · Geneva

N'Daba, Louis; Hodges-Aeberhard, Jane
HIV/AIDS and employment
Geneva, International Labour Office, 1998

/Comparison/, /AIDS/, /Discrimination against the disabled/, /Rights of the disabled/, /Personnel policy/, /Brazil/, /Côte d'Ivoire/, /France/, /Hungary/, /India/, /Indonesia/, /Jamaica/, /Mexico/, /South Africa R./, /Thailand/, /Uganda/, /USA/. 15.04.2
ISBN 92-2-110334-X

ILO Cataloguing in Publication Data

Printed in Switzerland

ART

CONTENTS

ACKNOWLEDGEMENTS

Many people were associated with this project and have provided valuable advice and assistance. We would first like to thank the authors of the country studies on which the information for this publication was based: Ms Ama Wattana (Thailand), the Hon. Justice Cameron (South Africa), Mrs M. Erskine (Jamaica), Mr. A. Grover (India), Dr T. Gyulavari (Hungary), Mr P. Lascoumes (France), Dr I. Lubis (Indonesia), Dr R.M.N. Nyonyintono (Uganda), Ms Panebianco Labbé (Mexico), Mr P. Petesch (United States), and Ms M.C. Pimenta de Oliveira (Brazil), as well as Ms. Evylene Chevalier and Ms Garance Upham who worked on the initial text. Second, we are grateful to Mr Mark Johnson who undertook preliminary editing with great practice and skill. Finally, the internal and external reviewers deserve special thanks for their valuable comments.

ABBREVIATIONS

ADA	Americans with Disabilities Act
AIDS	Acquired immunodeficiency syndrome
EEOC	Equal Employment Opportunities Commission
ERISA	Employee Retirement Income Security Act
FUE	Federation of Uganda Employers
GPA	Global Programme on AIDS
HIV	Human immunodeficiency virus
IEC	Information, education and communication
NGO	Non-governmental organization
SADC	Southern African Development Community
TBCA	Thailand Business Coalition against AIDS
UNAIDS	Joint United Nations Programme on HIV/AIDS
UNDP	United Nations Development Programme
USAID	United States Agency for International Development
WHO	World Health Organization

HIV/AIDS AND EMPLOYMENT

INTRODUCTION

1

Over the past ten years, the AIDS (acquired immunodeficiency syndrome) pandemic has continued to intensify and expand to affect all nations throughout the world. According to *UNAIDS Fact Sheet*, as at December 1996, 22.6 million people were living with HIV/AIDS, 2.1 million of whom were estimated as new HIV (human immunodeficiency virus) infections in 1996 alone. Table 1 shows its spread in the countries covered by this publication.[1] The population category that is worst affected is the 20 to 40 age group, which means that the active population (in the sense of the population that is of working age, and not only in the sense of "sexually active", an expression commonly used in connection with AIDS) is the worst affected age group, thereby giving rise, in addition to the individual's emotional and psychological trauma, to economic upheavals for society and problems in the world of work.

Table 2 gives more recent data at a regional level, as well as other information.

Although not contagious, HIV arouses fear, particularly where knowledge is lacking.[2] This fear, at times exploding into panic, results in discrimination in private life (in marriage, in the family), in civil society (in the community), as well as at the workplace. For people who are infected, discrimination occurs both in their attempts

Table 1.   Number of cases per 100,000 people in the countries studied

Country	AIDS cases	Date
United States	411 907	31.12.93
Brazil	49 312	26.02.94
Uganda	43 875	31.12.93
France	30 003	31.03.94
Côte d'Ivoire	18 670	24.02.94
Mexico	18 353	31.03.94
Thailand	5 654	14.06.94
South Africa	3 210	28.02.94
India	713	14.06.94
Jamaica	669	31.12.93
Hungary	149	31.03.94
Indonesia	49	14.06.94

Source: WHO/GPA annual document: *The world of HIV/AIDS: Actual situation at 1 July 1994*, Geneva, 1994.

to get jobs and keep them, and in their relationship with employers and colleagues. Media attention on the treatment of those infected with HIV has highlighted the extent of this discrimination.[3] It is therefore important to establish procedural and substantive guarantees in the labour market to ensure that infected workers enjoy full rights.

The international instruments created to combat discrimination (a) in society at large: the two International Covenants (on Economic, Social and Cultural Rights, and on Civil and Political Rights) of 16 December 1966 and (b) in employment and occupation: ILO Conventions, in particular the Discrimination (Employment and Occupation) Convention, 1958 (No. 111),[4] the Vocational Rehabilitation and Employment (Disabled Persons) Convention, 1983 (No. 159), and the Termination of Employment Convention, 1982 (No. 158)[5] — do not specifically refer to HIV/AIDS, as it had not been identified at the time of their adoption. Nor do they specifically refer to "medical conditions" as prohibited grounds for discrimination. Some commentators, inside and outside the ILO,[6] have called for an expansion of ILO instruments to cover HIV/AIDS.

Table 2. Regional HIV/AIDS statistics and features, December 1997

Region	Epidemic started	Adults and children with AIDS	Adult prevalence rate (%)[1]	Proportion of HIV-positive adults who are women (%)
Sub-Saharan Africa	Late 1970s - early 1980s	20 800 000	7.4	50
North Africa and Middle East	Late 1980s	210 000	0.13	20
South and South-East Asia	Late 1980s	6 000 000	0.6	25
East Asia and Pacific	Late 1980s	440 000	0.05	11
Latin America	Late 1970s - early 1980s	1 300 000	0.5	19
Caribbean	Late 1970s - early 1980s	310 000	1.9	33
Eastern Europe and Central Asia	Early 1990s	150 000	0.07	25
Western Europe	Late 1970s - early 1980s	530 000	0.3	20
North America	Late 1970s - early 1980s	860 000	0.6	20
Australia and New Zealand	Late 1970s - early 1980s	12 000	0.1	5
Total (rounded)		**30 600 000**	**1.0**	**41**

[1] The percentage of adults with HIV/AIDS in the adult population (15-49 years of age).

Source: UNAIDS/WHO: *Report on the global HIV/AIDS epidemic, December 1997,* Geneva, 1997.

For employers, the problem is to meet the challenge of managing their human resources in the best possible manner, while integrating the "AIDS risk" in their plans for developing their enterprise. When they are unable to develop an adequate response to this new challenge, whether due to a lack of knowledge, guidance or legal provisions to help them adopt measures and rational attitudes relating to employment, they often resort to improvised restrictive measures or, occasionally, a case-by-case progressive approach.

Where employers might expect to find technical assistance for the workplace, i.e. national AIDS programmes (usually centred in ministries of health), they can often obtain only generally worded policy statements and information on sporadic activities, frequently consisting of medical conferences and ad hoc group activities. Moreover, even when they are effective, national AIDS programmes cannot provide assistance to all the enterprises in the country: that is not their main function (coordination is) and they do not have the human or material resources to do so. When employers try to evaluate the present and future cost of HIV/AIDS for their business, they foresee a situation difficult to control.

Some employers' organizations have launched a collective response and have a clear vision of the essential role that can be played by enterprises in the prevention of HIV/AIDS. These initiatives have been adopted in the countries worst affected by the pandemic and are well known to international AIDS programmes. They involve research, assistance programmes and sensitization activities by non-governmental organizations (NGOs). However, this knowledge is not always shared with other employers' organizations. In an emergency situation, reinventing analyses, strategies and measures is a waste of time, resources and lives. The situation demands a more systematic approach to meetings and exchanges of experience, promoting economies of scale in spreading knowledge, and giving priority to disseminating results.

For workers, as for employers, the issue is the ability to work for as long as possible in fair and acceptable conditions. This involves, for both parties, learning to accept a new social obligation, namely the reduction of the HIV/AIDS risk. The community must also assume its responsibilities for the provision of medical care for infected workers, the management of their health and that of their families. Rejection and marginalization based on fear has to be banished and solidarity promoted. Interaction with colleagues with HIV/AIDS occurs at the everyday level in the office, classroom or workshop. This is the level at which support has to be provided, along with the maintenance of confidentiality.

Besides the individual behavioural changes that need to be adopted, challenges include the necessity of taking collective action to achieve greater social justice for people who are HIV-positive, including the right to full, freely chosen and productive employment.[7] What is at issue is a social phenomenon. Discrimination in employment on the grounds of being HIV-positive or having AIDS therefore has to become a new cause for workers' representatives. The adaptation of conditions of work for workers with HIV/AIDS has to be included in negotiations for the improvement of working conditions. Continuous training and education programmes must include accurate information on HIV/AIDS. Negotiations with employers should also cover the establishment of new sickness and survivors' insurance guarantees, or their inclusion in existing insurance schemes. State coverage also needs to be expanded. Finally, trade unions should conclude HIV/AIDS agreements with employers in the same way that wage agreements are concluded at national or sectoral levels.

Valuable experience has been gained in certain countries and by certain trade union organizations. As with employers' organizations, this information has to be widely disseminated so that it can be put to good use as rapidly as possible. This will then pave the way for the introduction of new measures and the transmission of results to others.

The International Labour Office is receiving an increasing number of requests for assistance and guidance in this field. Employers are requesting advice on measures to be taken in the enterprise. The Workers' Group of the ILO Governing Body, the World Health Organization (WHO)-chaired Inter-Agency AIDS Group (IAAG) and the United Nations Development Programme (UNDP), as well as eminent persons engaged in combating AIDS (such as the former Director of the Global Programme on AIDS, Dr. Jonathan Mann), have all asked the ILO to increase its HIV/AIDS-related activities.

In 1988, the ILO and WHO jointly signed a text which should serve as a point of reference at the international level concerning the principle of non-discrimination: namely the *Statement from the Consultation on AIDS and the Workplace* (see Annex II). It includes the essential elements of the policy to be followed on AIDS at the workplace. However, the ILO has not developed a mechanism for checking progress, nor has it been informed of the effect given to this Statement by its 176 member States. The Second International Consultation on HIV/AIDS and Human Rights, held under the auspices of the United Nations in September 1996, adopted 12 guidelines for States to implement an effective rights-based response to the spread of HIV/AIDS. Guidelines 5, 7 and 9 are relevant to this publication (see Annex III).

To assist in any such checking, the ILO's 1994-95 Programme and Budget included a research item to examine approaches to AIDS and employment, involving a survey of the law, collective agreements and practices in enterprises relating to the employment of people who are HIV-infected or have AIDS in a number of industrialized and developing countries. This study – executed over two years – consisted of two stages. The first comprised a series of national studies, based on replies to questionnaires from a number of different-sized enterprises[8] in the public and private sectors. The second was an international comparative analysis. Each of these stages had the aim, beyond that of adding to the information on the subject, of developing recommendations on policies for the workplace to provide broader protection for the employment of people with HIV/AIDS.[9]

For the international comparative survey, the ILO carried out research on 12 countries already identified by WHO data as having an AIDS problem, and with a geographical North-South spread in mind: Brazil, Côte d'Ivoire, France, Hungary, India, Indonesia, Jamaica, Mexico, South Africa, Thailand, Uganda and the United States. According to the WHO 1994 statistics for accumulated cases, a number of these countries are badly affected by the AIDS pandemic (Brazil, Côte d'Ivoire, France, Mexico, South Africa, Thailand, Uganda and the United States), while others are very little affected (Hungary and Indonesia). (Since that date, India has had to face up to a major HIV problem, and Jamaica has seen a substantial rise in HIV infections.)

The legal framework and enterprise practices in each of the countries were examined, as well as the level of HIV infection of the population, measured in terms of the rate of HIV infection of the sexually active adult population. Countries with a relatively low rate of infection have little motivation to establish regulations governing AIDS at the workplace. In contrast, countries with a high rate of infection have to adapt and develop their legal framework under the mounting visibility of the problem. Some countries that are not yet visibly affected by the pandemic have anticipated it, while others that are more severely affected have been slow to react.

There are evidently differences in the approaches adopted to AIDS, as on other matters, between industrialized and developing countries. The spread of HIV/AIDS is fuelled by inequalities of wealth, with Africa the continent that is worst affected. Indeed in Africa, AIDS, which in that continent's context is essentially a hetero-sexual disease, is above all synonymous with poverty and gender inequality. The situation there is compounded by the absence of social security, deficiencies in the health system and the failure to apply trade union rights, thereby missing the chance for worker and workplace involvement in the fight not only against the disease itself, but also against the discriminatory practices it engenders.

These differences in approach are analysed in both the first section of this publication, which deals with the legislative and regulatory framework, and the second section, which covers enterprise practices, from those that are judged to be negative, to those that are deemed to be more positive in terms of non-discrimination (e.g. codes of conduct on HIV/AIDS, HIV/AIDS agreements concluded in important industrial sectors). The third section contains an analysis of the impact of the measures that have been taken. The fourth section discusses the role of workers' and employers' organizations and the ILO, and proposes a number of recommendations for practical measures. Annex II offers a policy guide on measures that can be taken at the national level to prevent and combat discrimination in employment on the grounds of HIV infection or AIDS.

This publication is aimed not only at policy-makers, but also those who are faced with the daily challenge of eliminating direct or indirect discrimination against people with HIV/AIDS, such as enter-prise managers, representatives of employers' organizations, orga-nized and unorganized workers, infected people (whether or not they are members of an association) and voluntary activists in NGOs. The very nature of HIV/AIDS means that everyone has a role to play, not just scientific researchers and health care professionals, but every member of society, as part of his or her collective responsibility.

Notes

[1] The selection of these countries is discussed below.

[2] This point is made forcefully in Mann, J., Tarantola, D.J.M. and Netter, T.W. (eds.): *AIDS in the world: a global report,* Cambridge, Mass., Harvard University Press, 1992; Part II of which gives a useful epidemiological explanation and description of research into HIV.

[3] Newspaper accounts of the pandemic abound: see, for example, "Uganda meets AIDS crisis head on", in *Toronto Globe and Mail*, 23 June 1997, p. 5, and "South Africa's unmentionable curse", in *The Economist*, London, 5 July 1997, p. 45.

[4] The main provisions of Convention No. 111 appear in Annex I.

[5] Ratified by, respectively, 127, 59 and 28 member States of the ILO.

[6] Trebilcock, A.: "AIDS and the workplace: some policy pointers from international labour standards", in *International Labour Review*, Vol. 128, No. 1, 1989; Feldblum, C.R.: "Workplace issues: HIV and discrimination", in Hunter, W.D. and Rubenstein, W.B. (eds.): *AIDS Agenda*, New York, The New York Press, 1992; and ILO: *Equality in employment and occupation,* Special Survey of the Committee of Experts on the Application of Conventions and Recommendations, Report III (Part 4B), International Labour Conference, 83rd Session, Geneva, 1996, paras. 260-272 and 297.

[7] From Article 1 of the ILO's Employment Policy Convention, 1964 (No. 122); the Convention has been ratified by 88 ILO member States.

[8] The situations examined included the recruitment of people with HIV/AIDS, their conditions of employment and work, dismissals on the grounds of HIV infection or AIDS, assistance and social protection measures for infected workers, and training and information on preventive measures for the workforce as a whole. A number of national studies are supported by particularly complete practical information and can be consulted in their original language in ILO/NORMES/EGALITE, either by personal visit or in writing.

[9] It should be noted that for the specific cases of workers in high-risk exposure work environments, such as health care personnel and seafarers, which were not addressed in the study, reference should be made to the joint ILO/WHO: *Statement from the consultation on action to be taken after occupational exposure of a health care*

worker to HIV (Statement from the consultation on AIDS and the Workplace, Geneva, 1988 — Annex II to this publication*)* and the ILO/WHO *Statement on AIDS and seafarers,* Geneva, 5-6 October 1989. It should be noted also that, with regard to health care personnel, the Nursing Personnel Recommendation, 1977 (No. 157), calls for occupational health and safety conditions adapted to reducing the risk of exposure to special risks, which may be interpreted to cover the transmission of HIV. The Recommendation provides for financial compensation when nursing personnel are exposed to such risks.

THE LEGAL FRAMEWORK COVERING EMPLOYMENT OF PEOPLE WITH HIV/AIDS[1]

2

People who are HIV-infected or have AIDS need to benefit from general rights, such as the right to full, freely chosen and productive employment, the right to confidentiality as regards their HIV status and the right to social protection, including health care coverage. They also need to benefit from specific rights that accommodate the progressive decline in their capacity to work.

This examination of legislation relating to the employment of people with HIV/AIDS includes a review of the general provisions contained in constitutions and general legislation (civil codes and labour codes), as well as specific provisions, such as legislation to protect people with disabilities,[2] case-law relating to abusive dismissal on the grounds of HIV infection or AIDS, clauses contained in collective agreements, and measures with regard to health care professionals.

GENERAL LEGAL PROVISIONS

Even if general legal texts make no reference to infection with HIV or AIDS, people who are HIV-positive and enjoy full rights of citizenship in their country can use these general provisions if their general rights are violated and, as workers, can also claim social protection under general legal principles. In many constitutional law systems, non-citizens may also claim protection against contravention of these basic rights.

In some cases, the civil code provides protection against violations of privacy, while the labour code protects employees through proscription of discrimination on the grounds of health and unfair dismissal provisions.

Constitutions and civil codes:
Theoretical protection for equal rights

The universal principles of non-discrimination and respect for privacy, health and social security are contained in the Universal Declaration of Human Rights of 1948, which is based on the principle of equal rights. All States surveyed for the original study refer to the Universal Declaration in their Constitutions. In addition, several States prohibit any form of discrimination (Brazil, India, Mexico, South Africa[3]). The Constitutions of Brazil and Hungary establish the principle of respect for privacy. The Brazilian Constitution refers to the right to health and the Mexican Constitution provides for the right to social security. In the cases of France and the United States, no reference is made to the law at this general level, since there are specific laws directly protecting workers who are HIV-infected or have AIDS.

In the United States, the Civil Rights Act of 1991 (Title VII) can be used to file complaints concerning discrimination on the grounds of disability at the state or municipal levels with a view to obtaining damages with interest. In Mexico, the civil code states that confidentiality is an obligation placed upon doctors employed in enterprises.[4] In Brazil, the civil code covers employment in the private sector and the individual's right to privacy.[5]

Enforcement of constitutional rights is notoriously time-consuming and complex, thus people with HIV/AIDS who are involved in disputes relating to employment might prefer to turn to procedures laid down in labour legislation. This is particularly important for people who are HIV-positive, for whom any time that can be gained in the enjoyment of their rights is valuable.

Labour codes and regulations: Tools that need adapting

Anti-discrimination clauses

Even if texts do not specifically refer to HIV infection or AIDS as prohibited grounds for discrimination, labour codes often contain anti-discrimination clauses which implicitly cover this, such as those in France,[6] Hungary[7] and South Africa.[8] However, the usefulness of such provisions in enforcing the individual's rights is hampered by the fact that the burden of proving that the discrimination was based on HIV infection or AIDS lies on the infected worker.

Interestingly, in France, the penal (i.e. criminal) code recently supplemented the general principle set out in the civil code by introducing the concept of discrimination on the grounds of ill health and disability;[9] but the burden-of-proof issue remains, since the criminal standard of proof is stricter than the civil standard. In addition to the labour code, the provisions of general legislation have been developed in the form of the Charter of the National Council for the Prevention of Occupational Risks (1988) with regard to people who are HIV infected, a status which is not considered to be grounds for incapacity for employment. Moreover, if workers are declared incapable of working, they can appeal to the labour inspectorate.[10] In other cases, although workers who are under contract to the public service have a precarious status, it should be noted that workers who already show certain signs of AIDS have not only been recognized as capable of exercising their employment, but have been confirmed in their status as public officials.

In the United States, a major advance was registered with the adoption of the Americans with Disabilities Act (ADA), of 7 July 1990 (entering into force in stages between 1992 and 1994). However, there have been conflicts with previous legislation, which is still in force, namely the National Labor Relations Act and the Employee Retirement Income Security Act (ERISA) with regard to strategies to defend the interests of workers with HIV/AIDS. Before the adoption of the ADA, the courts found that the anti-discriminatory insurance provisions did not apply to cases of AIDS. This allows employers, in the context of self-insured health plans, to reduce coverage for people with AIDS. This issue has still not been resolved.

Recruitment and employment testing

Recruitment is usually subject to a medical examination in which the applicant has to be declared fit for the vacancy. The doctor is the only judge of the evaluation techniques to be used. For ethical reasons, HIV testing is theoretically excluded from the blood testing that may be required.

In Côte d'Ivoire, a non-restrictive schedule of diseases and grounds for incapacity for work is contained in the labour code. However, since the schedule does not include HIV status or AIDS, testing does not take place.

In Brazil, there is a very broad prohibition of testing, which also extends to the registration of students or workers for training in public or private educational institutions.

In Hungary, all tests that violate the right to privacy are prohibited,[11] and it may therefore be deduced that AIDS testing, both pre-recruitment and during employment, is prohibited. However, another provision appears to restrict this guarantee by stating that, before recruitment, both parties are bound by a mutual obligation of honesty. Does this mean that a worker who is HIV positive has to disclose this information to a potential employer? The question remains open. The labour code provides for the possibility of adopting specific rules governing requests for information in the event of a need to protect health.

In Mexico, pre-recruitment testing is not explicitly prohibited. Testing is sometimes authorized in a restricted manner for certain target groups. This occurs without amendment of the labour code, but rather through the adoption of ministerial regulations.

This is the case in India, where only staff of the national defence forces are currently subjected to regular pre-recruitment testing. The same practice is adopted by the South African Police Corps. Jamaican agricultural workers are submitted to the same test prior to working the harvest season in Canada.

Compulsory, clandestine and generalized testing occurs in some countries. For example, in Indonesia, a regulation issued by the Ministry of Labour and Migration authorizes pre-recruitment HIV testing for employment in occupational health services without the prior consent of the people concerned and, as a result, without counselling before or after the test. This discriminatory measure is explained by the fact that because HIV-positive status or AIDS is not included among the valid grounds for dismissal, it would be very difficult to dismiss an employee for this reason during employment.[12] In the United States, under the ADA, jobseekers who are HIV positive and who wish to benefit from the protection afforded by the Act must submit to an HIV test. When their HIV status has been recognized, no employer can refuse a job for this reason. However, workers benefiting from protection on the grounds of disability do not gain priority in access to employment.

During employment, the question arises as to whether annual testing may be included in routine medical examinations. Another question is that of the voluntary testing of workers who are considered to be at risk by the enterprise doctor. The concepts of capacity or incapacity for the job only apply at the level of the recruitment process. If sickness of whatever sort does not in general terms constitute grounds for the suspension of the contract of employment, it cannot be used as grounds for terminating the contract. This is true in Côte d'Ivoire, France and Uganda.

Nevertheless, restrictions exist in some countries, for example in Mexico, where the labour code obliges workers to submit to an annual medical examination;[13] special measures provide that a member of the armed forces who is infected with HIV shall be excluded from them.

Medical confidentiality

With respect to medical confidentiality and disclosure of HIV status in Mexico, the Federal Labour Act[14] makes it compulsory for workers who are infected with contagious diseases to inform their employers. However, this raises the question as to whether this concerns workers who are HIV infected or have AIDS, since HIV is transmissible, but not contagious.

Preventive measures

Prevention of HIV/AIDS at the workplace is also covered in some legislative texts of the countries studied. In Brazil, a national decree[15] makes it compulsory for enterprises to carry out internal preventive campaigns for the prevention of HIV/AIDS at the workplace. However, in Mexico the law makes it compulsory for workers to take preventive measures or follow procedures to prevent accidents or contagious diseases.[16]

Medical coverage

The legislative framework for medical coverage of infected workers and their dependants differs widely in the countries studied. In Indonesia, at one end of the spectrum, a regulation adopted by the Ministry of Labour and Migration[17] lays down that AIDS is not a disease that is covered by sickness insurance, as it is considered a disease that has been contracted intentionally by the individual. As such, it is classified under the same heading as drug and alcohol abuse. At the other end of the spectrum, the social security code in France, in addition to the labour code, contains provisions defining half-time work for therapeutic reasons and the accommodation of the workplace for workers who are HIV-positive and recognized as being disabled in the private and public sectors.[18] In Mexico, the public sector has to pay contributions to the social security system to finance medical coverage.[19]

In Côte d'Ivoire, another difficult situation arises since, on the death of a worker (whatever the cause), the regulations which govern entitlement to survivors' benefits do not take account of customary marriages.

Long-term sick leave which could help AIDS victims is recognized in only a few of the countries studied. In Mexico, in the public sector, authorized sick leave lasts for a maximum of 52 weeks. In order to benefit from this leave, employees have to have completed

14^1/$_2$ years of employment. This excludes the majority of workers with AIDS, who are often young people. In Côte d'Ivoire, after a first period of sick leave, if workers are still incapable of returning to work and their contract of employment is terminated for that reason, they become entitled to certain rights and benefits. Moreover, when they are replaced in the enterprise, they still have priority for re-employment for a period of one year (which can be renewed once). However, this measure would not appear well suited for people with AIDS. In France, in the public service, renewable leave for long illnesses amounts to three years (one year for contract workers). After these periods, officials may apply for early retirement if they have completed 15 years of service.

Current draft legislation covering the employment of people with HIV/AIDS

In addition to the provisions contained in constitutions, civil codes, labour codes and regulations, progressive new legislation on the employment of people with HIV/AIDS is being formulated in various countries. These draft texts are directly related to the subject of HIV/AIDS, or may in certain cases be used in an indirect manner to guarantee the right to employment of infected people.

In Brazil, the Medical Council of the State of Rio de Janeiro intends to make it compulsory for health insurance companies to cover all diseases, including HIV/AIDS. In Hungary, a draft text is in preparation to protect health data in health care establishments. Under this text, infected people will have to declare that they are HIV positive to the health service of an institution if they are requested to do so. This information will then be transmitted to the Central Health Register. The employer would not therefore keep information concerning the health of employees. Doctors are placed under the obligation of endeavouring to trace all those who could have been contaminated by the HIV-infected person and those who may have infected that person in the first place.

In Uganda, around 30 policy proposals have been put forward, although they do not constitute draft legislation as such. They might be adopted within the context of the national AIDS programme.

Proposals for the reform of the United States health care system, as regards allowances for workers, include amendments to the ERISA, which could strengthen the ADA (in contrast to the recommendations for reductions made by the Equal Employment Opportunities Commission — EEOC). There is a move under way, however, which has been criticized as helping stigmatize AIDS by national NGOs such as the AIDS Action Council and the National Association of People with AIDS. This is House of Representatives Bill No. 1062, introduced by a Republican Representative in 1996 and reintroduced on 13 March 1997, and is known as the HIV Prevention Bill.

The Bill:

- requires states to expand partner notification programmes to include anyone who may have been exposed to the virus;
- obliges states to keep central registries of all HIV infections (similar to states' existing registries of AIDS cases);
- expresses the "sense of Congress" that the information should remain confidential, but does not require states to ensure this;
- encourages – though not requires – states to make it a felony for a person to knowingly transmit HIV to another person;
- permits doctors to refuse treatment to any patient who refuses to take an HIV antibody test prior to an invasive medical procedure;
- requires a health care professional with HIV to inform the patient before performing any invasive medical procedure;
- compels persons accused of sex crimes to submit to HIV antibody testing, with the victim receiving the results of the test;
- drops federal Medicaid funding to states that do not comply with the legislation;
- obliges insurance companies that require applicants to take an HIV test as a condition for obtaining a policy to tell the applicant of the test results (a recent court ruling held that an insurer cannot be held liable in the AIDS-related death of an applicant because state law did not require notification); and

– allows people seeking to adopt a child to know the child's HIV status.

Another non-progressive legislative draft was the AIDS Prevention Bill submitted to the Indian Parliament in 1989. The Bill included discriminatory practices against people with HIV/AIDS, such as compulsory testing for people suspected of being infected, lifting confidentiality and placing such people in quarantine. The Bill was withdrawn by the Health Ministry in late 1991, apparently because of the fear that people would refuse to come forward for testing and because those found to be infected would be ostracized. It had reproduced the measures contained in the Public Health Act, 1985, as amended in 1987 of the State of Goa, an area suspected of being at high risk of HIV, since it is popular with tourists and AIDS is perceived in the country as being a foreign disease. Section 51 of the State Act requires notification of AIDS by medical practitioners who become aware that they are treating an HIV-infected person, while Section 53(1)(vi) permits HIV testing of people suspected of carrying the virus. People found to be seropositive may be isolated under specific conditions.

SPECIFIC LEGAL PROVISIONS AND JURISPRUDENCE

On the question of the protection of workers with HIV/AIDS other than through general provisions, a number of countries have adopted legislation extending the concept of disability to include people who are HIV positive. In other countries, court decisions have been favourable to workers when employment has been terminated on the grounds of HIV infection or AIDS. Clauses for the protection of HIV-infected workers have been included in a number of collective agreements, while specific measures have also been adopted for health care personnel.

Legislation on workers with disabilities

Traditional measures to protect the employment of people with disabilities can be used to cover HIV-infected people on the grounds of the progressive decline in their capacity for work. This approach involves measures to accommodate working time and make work easier, as well as issues relating to invalidity pensions. In these cases, employees have to reveal that they are HIV-positive, in the same way as workers who inform employers of their disabilities, in order to secure entitlement to certain rights.

In France, disability caused by infection with HIV is specifically included as an occupational disease for health care personnel only. There is a similarly restrictive approach in Mexico, where workers are recognized as being disabled in the case of non-occupational diseases only when they are permanently prevented from working. This does not therefore apply to people who are HIV-positive but who are still able to work on a part-time basis, or on a full-time basis with periods of sick leave. Moreover, public officials benefit from the provisions relating to permanent incapacity for work on the grounds of disability only when they have completed 14$^{1}/_{2}$ years of service. As mentioned above, young public officials, although more likely to have AIDS than older officials, are not therefore covered by these measures.[20]

In the United States, the ADA contains a broader approach. It extends the concept of disability to include people who are HIV infected or have AIDS, and as a result of a court decision, infection with HIV and AIDS have been specifically covered by the ADA since 31 October 1994.[21] Before then, people with HIV/AIDS were covered by the Rehabilitation Act, 1973, in particular Section 504.[22]

To benefit from the provisions of the ADA during employment, workers must have declared their disabled status, and therefore the fact that they are HIV positive, to their employer. They have to have been recognized as being "otherwise qualified", i.e. capable of fulfilling the essential functions of their job with or without accommodations at the workplace. Account is only taken of current capacity and not probable future capacity, although constant medical evaluation is nevertheless required. The ADA obliges employers, within the scope of their financial capacities, to make "reasonable accommodations" at the workplace for an employee who is HIV infected or has AIDS: the examples it lists in Section 10(a) include job restructuring, reassignment, adjustment of equipment and devices, modification of examinations and training modules, flexible working hours and additional sick leave. Employees who are at an advanced stage of AIDS and can no longer fulfil the essential functions of their job are covered by the social security system or their employer's private invalidity insurance. Under the United States social security system, people who are incapable of working are entitled to invalidity insurance allowances and to a supplementary security income. The social security system also includes certain measures to encourage people whose health status has stabilized to return to work.

With regard to recruitment, except for individuals who seek to become entitled to the protection of the ADA, testing for HIV is limited to cases in which occupational safety is at stake and to the evaluation of professional qualifications. Members of the families (parents or children) of people with disabilities are also covered by these measures. Third persons (health care personnel or people who assist the sick) benefit from the rights set out in the Family Medical Leave Act.

The ADA has been strengthened and interpreted by the guidance issued by the EEOC, which is responsible for its application. Thirty per cent of the cases under the ADA which come before the EEOC concern people who are HIV-infected or have AIDS. Legal actions brought under the ADA usually aim at reinstatement at work. In order to bring such actions, workers who are HIV positive have to pay the expenses of their lawyer and medical experts. However, lawyers' fees are not paid by plaintiffs who win their case, which considerably increases the cost of the financial penalty to employers for unjustified dismissal. However, despite these legal redresses, it is regrettable that there are no measures to simplify and expedite the procedures in cases submitted by HIV-positive workers because, besides the financial cost, time is precious.

Case-law on unjust dismissal on the grounds of HIV infection or AIDS

In a number of countries, progress has been made in the protection of the right to employment as a result of cases brought by workers who have been the victims of HIV/AIDS-related discrimination. For example, in Mexico, Article 123 of the Constitution permits the worker to choose between reinstatement and three months' severance pay; nevertheless, employers seem able to ignore the worker's choice of reinstatement following a Supreme Court ruling that the obligation to reinstate a worker is equivalent to an obligation that is impossible to execute by force. In Hungary, a British citizen residing permanently in the country is about to bring a case against his employer for discrimination on the grounds of AIDS. In Côte d'Ivoire, in July 1994, the Court of Appeal of Abidjan (further to a decision of the Labour Tribunal dated February 1993) found in favour of an agricultural wage-earner dismissed by his employer on the grounds that he was HIV-positive, although the Court refused to grant the damages and interest demanded by the dismissed worker.[23]

Also in July 1994, the Federal Employees Liability Act in the United States was used by a railway employee to bring a case for stress due to the fear of possibly having been infected with HIV while working in a dangerous area. (The employee was pricked by a discarded hypodermic needle with traces of blood when cleaning up an area frequented by drug addicts.) The Tennessee Supreme Court found in favour of the employee.

Under current case-law, a dismissal in France that is manifestly based on the HIV-positive status of an employee is not recognized as being lawful by the courts. An employer was found guilty by the Labour Tribunal (*Conseil de Prud'hommes*) of unjustified termination of a contract of employment (Bobigny, 24 October 1989). On appeal, the judgement was confirmed and the damages and interest relating to the moral injury were increased (Paris Appeal Court, April 1991). Two rulings by the Labour Tribunal (July 1990 and June 1994) and three rulings by Courts of Appeal (Aix, September 1992, and Paris, November 1992 and January 1993) have found dismissals on the grounds of HIV-positive status to be "lacking genuine and serious cause". Nevertheless, an employer can dismiss an employee whose sick leave, although shorter than the supplementary periods of compensation, disturbs the proper functioning of the enterprise by its frequency.

Collective agreements

When interpreted broadly, enterprise or sectoral agreements can sometimes support the position of an employee who is HIV infected or has
AIDS. They can be used to settle disputes relating to labour legislation
by granting more favourable conditions to infected workers. They also
provide a good reference point in the world of work regarding the
constraints resulting from an HIV-positive or AIDS status.

As regards sick leave, the question is whether repeated sick leave
absences, as with workers with HIV/AIDS, receive broader protection under collective agreements than under the general labour legislation. In France, collective agreements usually set out the general
conditions under which an employer can dismiss a sick worker. In
certain cases, only prolonged absence for reasons of sickness can
constitute a reason for terminating a contract of employment, and not
frequent and repeated absences. However, no specific agreements
regarding AIDS have been reported.

In Côte d'Ivoire, the Inter-Occupational Collective Agreement of
1977 makes no specific reference to AIDS, but does state that justified
absence from work (that is, absence resulting from sickness or a non-
professional accident) does not constitute grounds for termination of
employment, provided that it does not exceed six to eight months and
that it is supported by a medical certificate. Workers who are HIV-
positive and are treated by traditional medical practitioners (which is
increasingly the case in Côte d'Ivoire, due to health-related financial
issues) have experienced difficulties in producing a certificate whose
legal validity is recognized by the employer.

In the United States, the ADA covers both employers and trade
unions, in so far as a trade union cannot refuse membership to an
HIV-infected worker. Since the ADA does not make it compulsory
to adopt the best possible accommodation for the employment of
workers with disabilities (in this case, of those who are HIV-infected
or have AIDS), but rather "reasonable accommodations", there
should be no reason for conflict with collective agreements.
However, given the question of seniority, the issue of what should be
taken into account when defining a satisfactory accommodation is

being reviewed. Nevertheless, both Congress and the EEOC have recommended that clauses should be included in collective agreements allowing employers to take the necessary measures in accordance with the ADA. Negotiation requirements in the event of a complaint on the grounds of discriminatory practices in employment do not include direct dealing between the employer and the worker with the disability. Moreover, the ADA requires confidentiality for medical information to be lifted for managerial staff and directors of an enterprise, although this exception does not cover trade union representatives. Trade unions would appear to be covered by the same rules concerning confidentiality under the terms of the ADA where they are in receipt of medical data.

Very few collective agreements in the United States deal directly with HIV/AIDS, although commitments relating to non-discrimination, accommodations at the workplace, sickness benefits, disability leave, training and protective equipment have been included in six collective agreements. The agreements cover: hospital and health workers; the American Federation of State, County and Municipal Employees; the Hotel Employees and Restaurant Employees International Union; and public sector employees.

A trade union in the United States may also be forced to balance its position on reasonable accommodations between the interests of a disabled member (with HIV/AIDS) and other members concerned. If a trade union opposes a reasonable accommodation, a disabled member (with HIV/AIDS) can bring an action under the ADA against the union for failure to provide fair representation. Non-disabled members of trade unions may also take action against the union on the same grounds where the union supports accommodations that are more advantageous than seniority rights.

Finally, another situation which needs to be avoided under the terms of the ADA is one in which employers and unions could reach a deadlock if other employees panic, or go so far as to engage in a concerted refusal to work or to share equipment when advised of a case initiated under the ADA on behalf of a colleague with HIV/AIDS. A concerted refusal to work (for example, with a colleague who is

HIV infected) is possible under the terms of federal labour laws, whether the workforce is unionized or not. If a complaint is made under the Occupational Safety and Health Act, it has to be based on the possibility of imminent danger to health and safety, and must be objectively reasonable. This situation can be avoided if awareness-raising and AIDS education programmes are undertaken. It is for this reason that city councils in Chicago and Philadelphia have considered ordinances mandating workplace AIDS education. Recognizing the positive results of education efforts by private sector employees, in 1993 President Clinton ordered that all federal employees should receive HIV/AIDS training.

In South Africa, the Chamber of Mines of South Africa and the National Union of Mineworkers concluded a specific collective agreement in August 1993 covering HIV/AIDS (Annex IV). The agreement is exhaustive on many aspects of the question. It is rigorous in ethical terms and respects the interests of both parties. The agreement should therefore serve as a model beyond the mining sector and beyond South Africa. The objective of the agreement is to provide industry-level guidance: to minimize the effect of HIV/AIDS in the mining industry; to prevent the spread of HIV infection; and to develop the management of HIV infection in the employer/employee relationship. It includes a whole range of principles intended to permit the development of enterprise policies for HIV/AIDS, and sets in motion a process of permanent evaluation through a review of its provisions one year after its implementation or at any stage after that.

Such an agreement bears witness to the consensus achieved by the social partners on a highly controversial subject in a critical epidemiological context in a country where, until very recently, universal human rights had not been respected. It therefore constitutes proof, if any were needed, that private sector initiatives can lead to social progress in difficult situations.

Notes

[1] See also WHO/UNAIDS: *Directory of legal instruments dealing with HIV infection and AIDS: all countries and jurisdictions, including the USA*, Geneva, 1997.

[2] See also for a global overview of disability legislation the General Survey of the Committee of Experts on the Application of Conventions and Recommendations on Convention No. 159 and Recommendation No. 168, ILO: *Vocational rehabilitation of the disabled*, Report III (Part 1B), International Labour Conference, 86th Session, Geneva, 1997. A description of other legislation relevant to people with HIV/AIDS appears in Aeberhard-Hodges, J. and Raskin, C. (eds.): *Affirmative action in employment for ethnic minorities and persons with disabilities*, Geneva, ILO, 1997.

[3] The new Constitution (Republic of South Africa Constitution Act, 200 of 1993, Section 8(2)) specifies that this prohibition concerns employment in the public sector.

[4] Section 1943.

[5] Sections 1528 to 1532 and 159.

[6] Section L.120-2.

[7] Section 5 of the labour code.

[8] Labour Relations Act, No. 66 of 1995, in force from November 1996, S-187(1)(f) and Schedule 8 "Code of Good Practice: Dismissal", at Part 10 where reference is made to incapacity and ill health.

[9] Section 225/1.

[10] Section L.241-10.

[11] Labour code, Section 77.

[12] Act No. 12/1964 on dismissals.

[13] Section 134(10).

[14] Section 134(11).

[15] Decree No. 3/195/10-8-88.

[16] Federal Labour Act, Section 477(2).

[17] No. 18/4-1990.

[18] Act No. 07/94.

[19] Federal Labour Act for Public Employees, Section 43(VI)(b).

[20] Social Security Act, Section 128(2).

[21] The case of Kohn, Nast and Graf.

[22] For comment on the United States legal framework, see Parmet, W.E.: "An anti-discrimination law: necessary but not sufficient", Ch. 6 of Gostin, L.O. (ed.): *AIDS and the health care system*, New Haven, Connecticut, Yale University Press, 1990; and Mello, J.A.: *AIDS and the law of workplace discrimination*, Boulder, Colorado, Westview Press, 1995.

[23] Koffi v. Société Coco Service.

ENTERPRISE PRACTICES REGARDING THE EMPLOYMENT OF WORKERS WITH HIV/AIDS

3

In addition to the statutory and legal provisions that may exist concerning the employment of HIV-infected workers, it is necessary to examine actual workplace experience from the point of view of both employers and workers. Two main issues are of critical importance: the application of the labour law and the conditions under which work is accommodated to the specific needs of an HIV-infected worker in the normal environment. The workplace means both the public and private sectors. For the ten developing countries of the 12 countries covered by the original study, it is limited to urban employment in the so-called "modern" sector, thereby excluding the informal and rural sectors.

It has been difficult to collect examples perhaps because, in many cases, the impact of the epidemic has not been felt sufficiently in the field of work to be a cause of concern to the national economic actors. This comment applies to around half of the countries covered by this publication.

Negative enterprise practices

Fear of HIV/AIDS due to the lack of information, or to misinformation, against a background of economic and employment crises, leads to situations that are normally disastrous for workers infected with HIV. From compulsory testing, or at least testing for which consent has not been freely given, there is only one step to denial of access to employment or loss of employment, a step which is normally taken as a result of failure to respect medical confidentiality in the context of occupational medicine.

In view of these practices, employees are normally unaware of their rights and are traumatized by their health status. They therefore tend to adopt a passive attitude. Moreover, as a result of being rejected as victims, infected people run a greater risk of developing AIDS more rapidly, instead of "living positively"[1] and thereby extending their productive period by many years.

Under the heading of negative practices, three aspects are singled out. These are:

– the testing of workers upon recruitment and/or during employment;

– failure to respect medical confidentiality by health care personnel; and

– dismissal on the grounds of being HIV-positive or having AIDS.

The practice of concealing the existence of AIDS within the enterprise, although a serious aggravating factor, is not termed a negative practice in the study.

Testing of workers upon recruitment and/or during employment

In some countries, such as Indonesia, where testing during employment is considered ineffective, it is nevertheless used systematically prior to recruitment, particularly for the recruitment of seafarers to work on foreign vessels. In Mexico, it is reported that systematic testing is compulsory in large enterprises, frequent in medium-sized enterprises and the usual practice in the public sector. Only small enterprises do not resort to testing. The situation is worse in Côte d'Ivoire, where a labour inspector noted that testing prior to recruitment without the consent of the applicants is the general rule, from small to large enterprises. Reference is also made to the case of an agro-business enterprise in Abidjan, where verbal instructions from the management make this practice compulsory for the recruitment of managerial staff. In India, it was reported that one employer, out of the five who were interviewed, would impose pre-recruitment testing "where applicable": in the hotel industry, this enterprise stated that it only required medical reports on workers employed in the preparation of food. In South Africa, where testing is not the trend due to the non-discriminatory policy adopted by the principal group surveyed, one of the five enterprises covered by the study (in the chemical industry) nevertheless practises pre-recruitment testing under the worst possible conditions, namely where the result is not given to the applicant, but a full report on the medical examination is transmitted by the medical practitioner to the enterprise.

Non-respect of medical confidentiality[2]

Probably as a result of the absence of training on HIV/AIDS for medical staff in enterprises, but perhaps also as a result of the subordination of employees to their employers, which binds enterprise doctors to their employers, there are many cases in which the doctors' obligation to respect patient confidentiality – the Hippocratic Oath – is partially disregarded. Even beyond the issue of workers who are HIV infected or have AIDS, the confidentiality that should be observed for the medical files of individual staff members is frequently not respected. In Mexico, despite statements to the contrary, there is non-respect of confidentiality since personnel managers and even colleagues were reported to be informed of workers' infections. Furthermore, it appears that some of the laboratories which carry out the tests return the results to employers in the form of a list of names. In the Jamaican companies visited, medical files, which may include the results of HIV tests, are kept in the same place as other personnel information (CVs, evaluations, etc.). In Indonesia, the medical files of personnel are available to doctors, social assistants and managers in the four enterprises that were surveyed. In India, of the five enterprises surveyed, two do not guarantee the confidentiality of the files held in medical services or personnel departments. In Côte d'Ivoire, it seems that the non-respect of medical confidentiality might be explained by the fact that the medical responsibility of health care personnel is dominated by the hierarchical control of employers. It would appear that medical practitioners frequently directly inform the general management of the fact that an employee is HIV positive and are not sensitive when informing employers of the cost of any treatment to be borne by the enterprise and the diminished productivity of the employee.

The cases of the United States and France are very different, since their laws, which protect workers with HIV/AIDS, make it compulsory for the HIV status of employees to be disclosed to the employer so that the employees can benefit from their specific rights. Although this amounts to a breach of confidentiality, it is the voluntary decision of the infected worker and as such is not considered a negative practice.

Reference should finally be made to countries which, because of their rejection of testing, do not infringe the principle of confidentiality: Thailand and Uganda, countries that are heavily affected by the world pandemic.

Dismissal

From compulsory testing, reinforced by non-respect of medical secrecy within the enterprise, it is only a small step to the dismissal of workers who are HIV infected or have AIDS. Unfortunately, this step is taken in many countries, although apparently to varying degrees, since it is often very difficult to prove that the dismissal resulted from the discovery that the employee was HIV positive. In both developed and developing countries, economic reasons may be easily confused with the HIV-positive status of workers.

In Mexico, there are reports of many cases of dismissals, ostensibly due to the restructuring of enterprises, but in reality due to the workers' HIV status, of which they are not advised. Frequently, HIV-infected workers only learn of their HIV status from the management at the end of their contract. In other cases, the pressure and hostility against known HIV-infected workers force them to resign. When they do so, no compensation is paid and their social security entitlements are suspended.

In Côte d'Ivoire, it is reported that dismissals of workers who are HIV infected or have AIDS are an everyday occurrence (though one must bear in mind the high national incidence rate), although it seems never to be indicated that these are the grounds for dismissal. In many cases, the enterprise doctor suggests that the workers concerned should go and rest in their village and encourages them to leave their jobs through the payment of a bonus, the amount of which is determined by the head of personnel. Furthermore, the stigmatization at the workplace from colleagues can even extend to demanding the dismissal of a colleague who has AIDS.

In Jamaica, although the practice is a little different, it amounts to much the same. Enterprises request infected employees to go home until a solution has been found for them in their job. In so doing, they make it almost impossible for a return to work, in view of the very great psychological and social difficulties involved in their reintegration. Employers are then in a position to be able to pay rapidly the wages and medical compensation owed to the worker.

In Uganda, where non-discrimination at the workplace on the grounds of HIV/AIDS status is practised, certain enterprises that are members of the Federation of Uganda Employers (which is heavily involved in combating HIV/AIDS) have dismissed workers for "incapacity for work", which is in some cases related to their weakened state because they have AIDS. This is difficult to prove in the absence of trade unions in certain enterprises.

Similarly, although testing is not normally used in South Africa, the country's police force submits its members to pre-recruitment HIV testing and a case was reported where a police officer undergoing training was rejected from the Police Services on the grounds of being HIV infected and was given employment as a gardener. The test was not only compulsory, but had to be paid for by the applicant and was accompanied by no counselling services. Usually, people who are tested for HIV receive individual information and counselling before the blood test and a second counselling session when the result is announced, whatever the result.

In Hungary, almost half of the employers interviewed stated that they would dismiss an infected worker, but felt that the employee would most likely cease working on his or her own initiative. The

Chamber of Hungarian Physicians considers that practitioners who are infected should give up exercising their profession (although there is no legal obligation to do so). In addition, the Hungarian Army is under instructions to allow only HIV-negative recruits into its ranks and has to dismiss any soldier who is infected. In India, one out of the five employers surveyed envisaged the dismissal of infected workers.

POSITIVE ENTERPRISE PRACTICES

While some admittedly extreme and isolated examples have been described above, it should also be stated that the study found many admirable practices in all the countries examined, such as not dismissing a worker who is HIV positive. This is itself a progressive practice. Progressive cases also include those in which infected workers are able to stop working and benefit from adequate compensation and even assistance in terms of the moral, psychological, social, legal and medical help that a community can provide in order to enable them to live with the virus as well and as long as possible. However, because of labour law and the principle of non-discrimination in employment on the grounds of health, and because of the need for access to medical care, the special features of HIV infection and AIDS require the adaptation of conditions of employment. Furthermore, AIDS at the workplace is also an opportunity to adopt preventive educational policies for staff as a whole.

Compensation and assistance

The cases of France and the United States are again excellent examples of positive practices because the laws in both countries impose the adoption of a practice that combines therapeutic part-time work and compensation followed, as AIDS develops, by an invalidity pension. Moreover, all infected people who are covered by health insurance schemes are entitled to medical care.

Of the ten other countries covered by the survey, half have developed an approach under which infected workers benefit from the maintenance of their wages as they cease work and have access to medical coverage in the context of the national public health system. This is the case, for example, in Jamaica, where most workers who are HIV positive choose to remain at home in the knowledge that they will continue to receive their wages and health care reimbursements. In Thailand, HIV-positive workers whose symptoms develop and who require longer periods of sick leave than authorized by law are offered significant compensation and severance pay by their employers, far higher than the official minimum level. In Côte d'Ivoire, the nine enterprises surveyed all stated that they ensure medical coverage, including health insurance and hospitalization, and maintain the wages and acquired rights of workers with AIDS. However, the practical arrangements vary from generous coverage up to the end of the illness, regardless of cost, to situations where after the death of the worker the costs of medicines and hospitalization are deducted from the deceased's acquired financial rights that have to be paid by law to the survivors.

In Uganda, not only do employers generally refuse to dismiss workers who are HIV positive, but the Government has undertaken a real national and multi-sectoral community assistance system. Under the system, in banks, for example, employees who have AIDS receive more compensation than other sick employees. Elsewhere, employees even participate in therapeutical experiments and thereby benefit from increased assistance.

In South Africa, some enterprises do not provide on-site medical care, while the treatment of sick workers takes place outside the enterprise and is (with the exception of the drug AZT) covered by the enterprise's medical insurance scheme. Some have very well developed structures to cater for the needs of HIV-positive workers. One company operating mainly in the mining sector provides free health care to all workers who are HIV positive, whereas supervisory employees have to purchase a medical aid scheme. (However, neither of these schemes covers AZT.) Pre- and post-test counselling is provided at the enterprise, which is costly and time-consuming. Workers who develop a disabling disease (including AIDS) within six months of their employment are eligible for long-term disability benefits, based on a percentage of their wages and on the number of years worked. However, it is possible that benefits take so long to be processed that employees with AIDS may die before they can complete the formalities required to give up work. Some companies in the food retail sector put workers who are HIV-infected on permanent sick leave if they develop clinical AIDS. Hourly paid workers are covered by the industry sick fund, which pays their wages, and all basic primary care and standard medications are provided free. Premiums are deducted from the salaries of the staff.

Early retirement

This measure is mentioned, even though it does not concern the young people who are most likely to be affected by HIV/AIDS, because it is an option for HIV-infected employees who have completed a sufficient period of service to be able to take measures to ensure that their dependants benefit from the best material conditions after their death. In Thailand, infected workers who do not wish to continue working in the enterprise because of fear of having to reveal their HIV status or of no longer being able to hide it, may request early retirement. This is also the case when infected workers wish to spend their remaining time within their community. In the event of voluntary retirement, workers receive their acquired social security rights.

In Uganda, in the hotel industry, when AIDS has become far advanced, workers are notified that they can take retirement while benefiting from full financial benefits. In banks, HIV-positive employees can retire early and invest their entitlements for as long as they are strong enough to benefit from them. In South Africa, in certain enterprises in the chemical sector, a worker who develops AIDS can apply to receive retirement benefits and an invalidity pension.

Accommodation of the workplace and working time arrangements

It should be recalled that the time between the onset of HIV infection and the development of clinical AIDS, or at least up to the final stages when a worker has to cease work, frequently ten years, is sufficiently long for infected workers to be able to retain their jobs. However, in view of their gradual deterioration in health, they need to take periods of sick leave that become longer; they also suffer from physical and psychological problems that are increasingly disabling. This means that it is necessary to adapt the working environment and job content to the progression of the disease.

Reference is made to such measures in one half of the national case-studies, namely those covering countries that have not enacted legislation respecting workers with disabilities (including HIV/AIDS). One such instance is the hotel industry in Uganda, where workers with "infectious" diseases (whatever they may be) are transferred from so-called sensitive jobs (in such fields as food handling and restaurants) to other less sensitive work (such as laundry or house-work). In Ugandan banks, when AIDS symptoms become evident, infected workers are taken from their posts so as not to worry clients and to avoid the infected workers suffering from any possible nega-tive reactions from clients.

In South Africa, some food retail companies guarantee that workers infected with HIV are retained in their job following its adaptation. In the mining sector, where there might not be the tech-nical capacity to provide less arduous work to infected employees, workers are encouraged to take leave for permanent incapacity. There have been cases in the South African chemical sector of HIV-positive lorry drivers who transport chemical products being trans-ferred to less dangerous work, although this work requires lower skills at lower wages, owing to the lack of the risk bonus. In Côte d'Ivoire, one third of the enterprises surveyed stated that they reclassify HIV-infected staff, who keep the same wage levels and acquired rights.

There remains the case of India, in which the only examples of practice involved statements of intent by some companies. Less than half indicated that they were in favour of maintaining infected workers in employment through the adaptation of the workplace, but over half supported the accommodation of the workplace, either by reducing working time or decreasing the amount of work.

The ADA and French legislation concerning people with disabilities provide a real arsenal of measures for the ergonomic accommodation of jobs, as well as very strict rules concerning the variable duration of working hours. American workers who are HIV-infected are treated in the same way as workers suffering from other incurable diseases, such as cancer or heart disease. French enterprises that do not wish to give effect to the relevant measures have to pay a penalty. While it is true that occupational reclassification, reductions in working hours and the adaptation of work content may be a source of jealousy for other employees, the ADA does provide for a sophisticated balancing of the interests of management, the infected employee and the union, including joint interests such as the need to preserve the financial viability of any health and welfare fund or of benefits for all contributors.

Education campaigns

This is a subject that would merit a whole study in itself in view of the wealth of information gathered at the national level. This publication confines itself to summarizing the various types of initiatives taken at the workplace to combat the HIV epidemic and prevent its spread to the non-infected workforce.

It is remarkable that, despite the inequalities of resources available to the various social actors in different national situations, countries as different as South Africa and the United States both have employers who are also efficient in the "art" of talking about AIDS at the workplace. It should be noted that even a country such as Jamaica, where the rate of HIV infection was until recently very low, has adopted a multi-sectoral strategy to combat AIDS at the workplace.

It is clear that distinctions need to be made in assessing the impact of the action described below, such as whether workforces are organized, whether they are affiliated to an employers' organization that is active in this field, the sizes of enterprises, whether national AIDS programmes are active at the workplace, and whether partnerships with specialized NGOs are in place.

First, enterprises can often seek external support, from national AIDS programmes or NGOs, in training instructors, carrying out studies and evaluations, and undertaking anonymous and free testing (with pre- and post-test counselling). Second, internal measures can be applied, including: official commitment by the management; commitment by trade unions; talks by occupational doctors; distribution of condoms; establishment of AIDS committees and services for sexually transmitted diseases/HIV/AIDS; peer education; and knowledge, attitude and practice surveys.

Third, the training materials that are used vary enormously and often reflect sensitivity to local customs and restricted resources: use of local languages (particularly for illiterate women); talks by people infected with HIV; audiovisual materials; and animation activities such as street theatre and songs. The actual materials can vary from the traditional teaching techniques of posters, stickers and enterprise newsletters to T-shirts and caps with slogans, as well as comic strips and condoms.

Fourth, many campaigns use community counselling. Although this practice is not, properly speaking, a prevention measure, it forms part of the same approach by, for example, providing an opportunity for people to express their fear of AIDS, communicate confidentially and break their isolation. It involves training a psychological counsellor at the enterprise or calling in skilled external services. The objective is to provide an opportunity for workers who are infected or have come into contact with HIV/AIDS to express themselves within their own community, enterprise, unit or residential area. This moral and emotional assistance is essential to enable people to live better with HIV/AIDS.

Commitment in the form of a code of conduct

A code of conduct is one of the best guarantees when legislation is inadequate. Proof of this is the adoption, in 1997, of the regional code on AIDS and employment of the Southern African Development Community (SADC), following several workshops in the early 1990s on approaches to AIDS awareness in the 12 countries constituting the

SADC. At the national level, such codes amount to a national contract binding employers' and workers' organizations to apply the same rules with regard to the employment of people with HIV/AIDS.

Of the countries researched for this publication, only South Africa provides an illustration of this type of positive practice, namely the code developed in August 1995 for the South African National Economic Development and Labour Council. Moreover, as an indication of the real mobilization in South Africa on this subject, another code has been produced by Business South Africa.

Codes of this type usually contain recommendations on the following subjects: HIV/AIDS and the contract of employment (recruitment and/or renewal, training and promotion, health and sick leave); special allowances and related benefits; disputes and disciplinary procedures; HIV/AIDS education (responsibilities of the employer/employee); testing; confidentiality; fear among colleagues at work and the management; management of health care; and support and counselling at the workplace.

Notes

[1] The slogan adopted by NGOs of infected people, and particularly the AIDS Service Organization TASO, in Uganda.

[2] The testing of workers in relation to labour codes and regulations has been referred to in the section on recruitment and employment testing in Chapter II above.

THE ROLE OF EMPLOYERS' AND WORKERS' ORGANIZATIONS

4

IDEAS AND ACTIONS INTRODUCED BY EMPLOYERS AND THEIR ORGANIZATIONS

In addition to the many constraints facing managers of modern enterprises, these people now have to cope with a new factor, namely the management of the AIDS risk over the next five to ten years. A long-term policy cannot be based on dealing with the problem on a case-by-case basis, involving the provision of assistance to infected workers, or the extremes of dismissal of infected workers and testing (whether or not it is confidential) prior to recruitment; even information, education and communication (IEC) programmes for prevention may not be enough.

The examples in this publication show that employers can deal better with the problem, irrespective of their country of operation, by adopting a rational, planned and collective approach.

In view of the experiences described, a determining factor appears to be the development by employers' organizations at the national level of policy guidance concerning AIDS at the enterprise, even before proposals are made by national AIDS programmes. The most innovative enterprises in adopting approaches to combat AIDS, both in terms of prevention and assistance, are reference points for disseminating knowledge and producing multiplier effects. To succeed in these aims, a genuine policy has to be launched for the training of managers in evaluating the impact of HIV/AIDS on their enterprises.

A model example of corporate HIV policy was developed in New England, United States, when, in 1989, nine large employers joined together to form the New England Corporate Consortium for AIDS Education. The mission of the consortium was to provide leadership and advocacy, in the business community on workplace HIV issues including education, public policy, community relations, and corporate philanthropy. This consortium, which originally consisted of Bank of Boston Corporation, Bank of New England, Cabot Corporation, DAKA International, Digital Equipment Corporation, Lotus Development Corporation, New England Telephone, Polaroid Corporation, and TEXTRON, developed ten principles for workplace policy relative to HIV. Each of these companies adopted these principles and the consortium encouraged several hundred companies nationwide to adopt them as well.

These principles are as follows:

1. Persons with HIV infection, including AIDS, in our company have the same rights, responsibilities, and opportunities as others with serious illnesses or disabilities.

2. Our employment policies comply with federal, state, and local laws.

3. Our employment policies are based on the scientific facts that persons with HIV infection, including AIDS, do not cause risk to others in the workplace through ordinary workplace contact.

4. Our management and employee leaders endorse a non-discrimination policy.

5. Special training and equipment will be used when necessary, such as in health care settings, to minimize risks to employees.

6. We will endeavour to ensure that AIDS education is provided to all of our employees.

7. We will endeavour to ensure that education takes place before AIDS-related incidents occur in our workplace.

8. Confidentiality of persons with HIV infection and AIDS will be protected.

9. We will not screen for HIV as part of pre-employment or workplace physical examinations.

10. We will support these policies through their clear communication to all current and prospective employees.

Two further illustrations of forward-looking corporate HIV policy are provided by the Federation of Uganda Employers (FUE) and the Thailand Business Coalition against AIDS (TBCA). These two countries of the South, with some of the highest rates of HIV infection worldwide, and in the absence of any specific legal obligations respecting the employment of workers with HIV/AIDS, have some of the most specific guidance from employers' organizations (which also appears to be well adapted to their own circumstances).

The FUE is a private non-profit-making association, representing a total of 140 private and semi-public enterprises that employ 400,000 employees. In 1988, with the support of the United States Agency for International Development (USAID), it introduced an IEC programme on AIDS for a two-year period. The logistical support from USAID made it possible for the FUE to adapt its existing health and safety programme and create its own AIDS programme, a pioneer at the international level. The objective of the programme is to encourage a change in the sexual behaviour of staff so as to reduce their risk of acquiring HIV. The specific objectives of the programme include: an increased level of knowledge about HIV/AIDS by the workplace population (the transmission of skills, particularly in the use of condoms and the adoption of safer sex habits); a positive attitude among workers towards infected people; and support for the development of enterprise AIDS policies. This peer-education strategy, implemented by FUE trainers and disseminated through many training materials, has achieved encouraging results. Between 1988 and 1993, over 150,000 workers were reached and more than 2.5 million condoms distributed. The level of knowledge has increased significantly and a change in sexual behaviour is perceptible.

The TBCA is also a non-profit-making association. Set up in the private sector by Thai and foreign employers, its objective is to develop a response to HIV/AIDS by employers in terms of the formulation of appropriate enterprise policies and education programmes for employees at the workplace. The target populations of TBCA activities range from enterprise managers to workers. TBCA carries out three types of activities: managing and coordinating AIDS training and education; holding various types of training workshops; and preparing and distributing a manual and a quarterly bulletin of AIDS information. A TBCA guide is published in English and Thai in straightforward language. It includes guidance for the development of education programmes that are adaptable to each enterprise. It also contains tools for the evaluation of needs and proposed policies. It lists many addresses of institutions combating AIDS that may be useful to employers.

An employer has to be able to develop and offer specific training modules to staff for HIV/AIDS awareness. For this, the best trainers on this subject are the staff themselves and peer education is therefore recommended at all levels. This presupposes that HIV/AIDS is included in the enterprise's annual training plan. Time has to be set aside for the training and education of instructors. These instructors need to be freed from their work responsibilities during the training sessions to facilitate in them an intensive and in-depth ability to transmit knowledge and to enable them to acquire specialized skills in transmitting knowledge on sensitive subjects (sex and death). The second stage is further training, mainly at the individual level. Sufficient time has to be made available for this activity. The target populations usually include managerial and supervisory staff and workers.

Another element in the impact of employers' ideas and actions is the attention paid to health insurance and pensions. Medical expenses could be reimbursed to the extent possible for workers with HIV/AIDS and their families through sickness and survivors' group insurance schemes. In developed countries, the social security system, and particularly the protection guaranteed as a result of the invalidity status accorded to workers with HIV/AIDS, frees enterprises from playing a direct social assistance role. Nevertheless, the increase in insurance premiums as the pandemic progresses is a growing problem. In developing countries, too few major enterprises have taken out group insurance schemes for their staff. They could be encouraged to do so through an emphasis on the long-term viability of such investments. Employers' organizations should provide guidance and, where appropriate, negotiate with insurers. It is true, however, that the financing of health care schemes that cover people who are HIV infected and have AIDS will become an increasingly heavy burden on social contributions. One way of lightening this burden could be a policy of incentives for early retirement to create a balance between the two schemes. Early retirement is a humane and economic solution that employers could be encouraged to adopt.

Likewise, in the field of occupational medicine there is a place for employer initiatives. Investing in health care personnel to cope with the impact of HIV/AIDS also means giving effect to laws that require the presence – constant or temporary – of a doctor at the enterprise. Employers' organizations could provide guidance in this respect and bring pressure to bear so that this cost is counted as part of the global effort that needs to be made to combat AIDS and be remunerated. However, the employment of a doctor should not mean that employers could then claim to have an influence over medical confidentiality. Developments in legal provisions and their application will undoubtedly lead to the adoption of more severe sanctions at this level.

Another idea could be that employers' organizations arrange inter-enterprise training seminars for health care personnel and doctors in enterprises.

IDEAS AND ACTIONS INTRODUCED BY WORKERS AND THEIR ORGANIZATIONS

Whether or not workers are aware that HIV/AIDS is a threat to everyone, they are globally the most exposed category in view of the age range of those most commonly affected (15 to 40). Fear resulting from lack of information or misinformation on the characteristics of HIV/AIDS leads to a rejection of the subject and of infected people, who are also badly informed and often react by isolating themselves and hiding their HIV status. Nevertheless, the world of work has to be considered as a community that needs to be wholly preserved from intolerance. The workplace has to become the main centre of community action, whether as training, assistance or prevention. It is essential, therefore, that everyone should be provided with precise and clear information on matters relating to HIV infection and AIDS. To contain the spread of the virus, it is necessary to disseminate educational messages through the best available channels, that is, natural leaders, workers' representatives, popular trainers and community leaders.

Trade union mobilization, as the case of the South African National Union of Mineworkers showed, can be crucial.[1] Major subregional activities have also been taken over the past few years by the Organization of African Trade Union Unity in the training of trade union leaders as part of its Health, Safety and Environment Programme, based in Harare, and carried out with the ILO. In addition, the national activities undertaken by the Zambia Congress of Trade Unions (seminars, workshops and training for occupational safety and health committees at workplaces) in the fields not only of training, but also of counselling and assistance to infected workers, are highly appreciated both at the workplace and in the community at large, and are excellent examples of a great impact with limited resources.

Another purposeful effort was the HIV/AIDS educational programme launched by the Zimbabwe Congress of Trade Unions in 1992. This programme formed part of the activities of its Health and Social Welfare Department. It later held an evaluation workshop with the participation of trainers and peer educators from the affiliate unions to assess the HIV/AIDS programme. Various signs that the programme was having an impact included the following:

– trainers and peer educators carried out their activities in their workplaces;

– those trained also educated other groups in churches, burial societies, clubs and families;

– HIV/AIDS drama groups were formed in all regions;

– union education departments included HIV/AIDS in their programmes;

– some unions established drop-in centres to discuss HIV issues; and

– tripartite and bipartite meetings were held to discuss HIV/AIDS policy.

With regard to the protection of workers with HIV/AIDS in the framework of disputes on the grounds of discrimination, there might be cases where it is difficult to obtain the support of a trade union. This is despite the necessity of adopting collective approaches to the right to employment and to defend employment at a time of crisis and generalized unemployment. Moreover, in many countries, there are no active trade unions or institutions to defend human rights.

Workers' education programmes could train trade unionists, as the representatives of workers, to become community leaders in the fight against HIV/AIDS and to become partners of employers in preventing AIDS and assisting HIV-infected people. Infected workers themselves need to be trained in how to deal with their HIV-positive status. They can become educators. They are also partners of the employer, benefiting from the accommodation of their working conditions, and even early retirement. In addition, workers who are not infected need to be educated about HIV/AIDS, either inside or outside workers' organizations. They too can become educators and counsellors.

Workers' representatives could assume a more assertive role in negotiating realistic conditions with employers for enterprise HIV/AIDS agreements. To do so, they must adapt prevention and solidarity messages to the culture of each category of workers, emphasize the role of voluntary leaders in multiplying the dissemination of information, and extend education activities to workers' families.

Mention should also be made of another category of workers exposed to HIV in their work, but who are referred to less frequently, namely, commercial sex workers. Although they are not governed by the same labour provisions as discussed earlier, trade unions nevertheless exist, particularly in Latin America and Asia, and they are actively engaged in combating AIDS.

THE INTERNATIONAL COMMUNITY AS A WHOLE AND THE ILO

The ILO has an important role to play in HIV/AIDS in a number of ways. This is because without important measures, the current HIV epidemic may reach the stage of a mass AIDS epidemic, and there are grounds to fear a loss of control by governments of their national economic machines. Such measures include learning to manage the cost of HIV/AIDS at the enterprise, investing in prevention, and planning for the cost of assisting infected workers. The ILO, it is true, could do more in supporting HIV/AIDS training policies for employers through a role of catalyst in: offering pilot programmes on HIV/AIDS and employment to employers' organizations; holding seminars for the exchange of experience at the national, regional and global levels;[2] and designing and publishing materials adapted to employers, and disseminating those that already exist. The ILO could also play a significant role through addressing HIV/AIDS in its workers' education programme. Indeed, the Bureau for Workers' Activities of the ILO already has a section on HIV/AIDS in its modules for training of unionists.[3] These modules provide basic information on AIDS – including discussion on why it is a trade union issue – and on HIV – namely, modes of transmission, methods of prevention and policy issues. Discrimination in the workplace is discussed, as is the HIV/AIDS role of the health and safety representative in the workplace.

In addition, a new publication of the Bureau for Workers' Activities and the Labour Law and Labour Relations Branch devotes a section to advising unions how to negotiate for appropriate HIV/AIDS information and health education, including counselling for workers and families exposed to HIV/AIDS.[4] It explains which workers may be at increased risk because of their work. It also discusses how exposure to HIV/AIDS can be prevented in occupations where there is a potential risk of exposure. In brief, workers should be provided with education in the methods of prevention; a written policy stating what to do and whom to contact in case of exposure should be developed in all workplaces where workers may be exposed to blood or other bodily fluids; and workers should be familiar with the policy which should be posted where everyone can see it. In addition, it lists issues to be considered in the development of a workplace policy on HIV/AIDS, such as:

– pre-employment screening;

– HIV/AIDS screening for employed workers;

– confidentiality;
– informing the employer;
– protection of the employee;
– access to services for employees;
– benefits;
– reasonable changes in working arrangements;
– continuation of the employment relationship;
– first aid; and
– prevention of victimization.

All these activities could feed into national AIDS programmes, where they exist.

As an alternative to continued work in the enterprise, individual or community income-generating activities could be encouraged so that workers infected with HIV but not yet facing clinical AIDS can be retrained and therefore maintain their families and build up life insurance in countries where there is no social security system. Projects to support these activities, and the training of workers with HIV/AIDS in entrepreneurship and management, should be encouraged by the ILO in the same way that projects of this type have been developed successfully for people with other disabilities.

The ILO has a potential role as an institutional actor in combating HIV/AIDS through training employers' organizations and trade unions; it could also play a role in advising governments and setting a framework for standards on the employment of workers who are HIV infected or have AIDS. The 1988 joint ILO/WHO *Statement from the Consultation on AIDS and the Workplace* (Annex II) could be disseminated further. This publication in a way constitutes a small first step in putting forward examples of already existing approaches.

Finally, the ILO could encourage more active use of Convention No. 111, as pointed out by the Committee of Experts,[5] if the criterion of state of health were to be added to the text by a protocol.

Notes

[1] This was pointed out in the report — *The role of the organized sector in reproductive health and AIDS prevention* — of the ILO's tripartite workshop for English-speaking Africa, held in Kampala, Uganda, in November/December 1994.

[2] Along the lines of the tripartite workshop held in Uganda, mentioned above.

[3] ILO: *Your health and safety at work: A collection of modules*, Geneva, 1996.

[4] Olney, S., Goodson, E., Maloba-Caines, K. and O'Neill, F.: *Gender equality: A guide to collective bargaining of working conditions,* Geneva, ILO, 1998.

[5] ILO: *Equality in employment and occupation,* Special Survey of the Committee of Experts on the Application of Conventions and Recommendations, Report III (Part 4B), International Labour Conference, 83rd Session, Geneva, 1996, paras. 260-272 and 297.

FINAL COMMENTS

5

In undertaking the original study, the International Labour Office demonstrated its commitment to engage in reflection on a new and topical subject, namely the response of the world of work to the humanitarian challenge of the end of the twentieth century – HIV/AIDS.

For the ILO, addressing the issue of the employment of workers who are HIV-infected or have AIDS responds to the need to disseminate examples of current workplace practice so as to be ready to answer potential requests for assistance from Ministries of Labour, Training and Health, as well as from workers' and employers' organizations. It also responds to the concern of jurists, occupational doctors, human resource advisers and to the anguish of people with AIDS, whether or not they exercise an occupational activity. Finally, it responds to the calls made by other international organizations involved in the global strategy to combat HIV/AIDS.

This examination of the legislative framework, collective agreements and codes of practice covering the world of work as they relate to HIV/AIDS provides reference points that can be used for the development of suitable legal measures. Although observance of occupational medical confidentiality and the right to information and prevention are universal concepts, the protection of workers with

HIV/AIDS, through the recognition of their status as disabled workers, would appear to be an approach adapted to the context of industrialized countries. Despite the different approaches adopted, the enactment of specific national legislation covering the employment of infected people provides a basic universal guarantee.

The social partners and civil society have to be able to mobilize in order to develop and apply these measures. The ILO should endeavour to assist them through its legal and its training expertise. The joint ILO/WHO *Statement from the Consultation on AIDS and the Workplace*, for example, needs to be broadly disseminated in all countries, as it can provide a basis for technical training measures for jurists, counsellors, doctors, trade unions, employers' organizations and associations of people with HIV/AIDS.

The examination of enterprise practices with regard to the employment of workers who are HIV infected or have AIDS shows the broad disparities between the responses at the workplace to the challenge of HIV infection. The study highlighted two categories of positive approaches, namely those adopted in a strong legislative framework (France and the United States) or social environment (Thailand and Uganda), as well as successful actions in a general environment of attentiveness to the subject (Hungary, Jamaica and South Africa). The study also identified some of the negative discriminatory practices (such as those identified in certain sectors in Brazil, Côte d'Ivoire, India, Indonesia and Mexico) so as to combat them in future.

The willingness of employers and workers to take action should be enshrined in multi-sectoral national policies to combat AIDS. It is necessary to promote private sector initiatives on an urgent basis and to undertake AIDS training (prevention and community assistance) at the workplace. It is also indispensable for the public sector, which is still the major provider of salaried employment in developing countries, to develop the resource structures for the dissemination of a permanent message of solidarity among public employees. For activities of this magnitude and urgency, major political awareness and commitment are vital. It is hoped that this publication will give all actors on the social scene something to consider in this direction.

ANNEXES

ANNEX I

INTERNATIONAL LABOUR CONVENTION AND RECOMMENDATION CONCERNING DISCRIMINATION IN RESPECT OF EMPLOYMENT AND OCCUPATION

Discrimination (Employment and Occupation) Convention, 1958 (No. 111)

The General Conference of the International Labour Organisation,

Having been convened at Geneva by the Governing Body of the International Labour Office, and having met in its Forty-second Session on 4 June 1958, and

Having decided upon the adoption of certain proposals with regard to discrimination in the field of employment and occupation, which is the fourth item on the agenda of the session, and

Having determined that these proposals shall take the form of an international Convention, and

Considering that the Declaration of Philadelphia affirms that all human beings, irrespective of race, creed or sex, have the right to pursue both their material well-being and their spiritual development in conditions of freedom and dignity, of economic security and equal opportunity, and

Considering further that discrimination constitutes a violation of rights enunciated by the Universal Declaration of Human Rights;

adopts this twenty-fifth day of June of the year one thousand nine hundred and fifty-eight the following Convention, which may be cited as the Discrimination (Employment and Occupation) Convention, 1958:

Article 1

1.   For the purpose of this Convention the term "discrimination" includes —

(a)   any distinction, exclusion or preference made on the basis of race, colour, sex, religion, political opinion, national extraction or social origin, which has the effect of nullifying or impairing equality of opportunity or treatment in employment or occupation;

(b) such other distinction, exclusion or preference which has the effect of nullifying or impairing equality of opportunity or treatment in employment or occupation as may be determined by the Member concerned after consultation with representative employers' and workers' organisations, where such exist, and with other appropriate bodies.

2. Any distinction, exclusion or preference in respect of a particular job based on the inherent requirements thereof shall not be deemed to be discrimination.

3. For the purpose of this Convention the terms "employment" and "occupation" include access to vocational training, access to employment and to particular occupations, and terms and conditions of employment.

Article 2

Each Member for which this Convention is in force undertakes to declare and pursue a national policy designed to promote, by methods appropriate to national conditions and practice, equality of opportunity and treatment in respect of employment and occupation, with a view to eliminating any discrimination in respect thereof.

Article 3

Each Member for which this Convention is in force undertakes, by methods appropriate to national conditions and practice —

(a) to seek the co-operation of employers' and workers' organisations and other appropriate bodies in promoting the acceptance and observance of this policy;

(b) to enact such legislation and to promote such educational programmes as may be calculated to secure the acceptance and observance of the policy;

(c) to repeal any statutory provisions and modify any administrative instructions or practices which are inconsistent with the policy;

(d) to pursue the policy in respect of employment under the direct control of a national authority;

(e) to ensure observance of the policy in the activities of vocational guidance, vocational training and placement services under the direction of a national authority;

(f) to indicate in its annual reports on the application of the Convention the action taken in pursuance of the policy and the results secured by such action.

Article 4

Any measures affecting an individual who is justifiably suspected of, or engaged in, activities prejudicial to the security of the State shall not be deemed to be discrimination, provided that the individual concerned shall have the right to appeal to a competent body established in accordance with national practice.

Article 5

1.   Special measures of protection or assistance provided for in other Conventions or Recommendations adopted by the International Labour Conference shall not be deemed to be discrimination.

2.   Any Member may, after consultation with representative employers' and workers' organisations, where such exist, determine that other special measures designed to meet the particular requirements of persons who, for reasons such as sex, age, disablement, family responsibilities or social or cultural status, are generally recognised to require special protection or assistance, shall not be deemed to be discrimination.

... [Articles 6 to 14 - standard final provisions]

Discrimination (Employment and Occupation) Recommendation, 1958 (No. 111)

The General Conference of the International Labour Organisation,

Having been convened at Geneva by the Governing Body of the International Labour Office, and having met in its Forty-second Session on 4 June 1958, and

Having decided upon the adoption of certain proposals with regard to discrimination in the field of employment and occupation, which is the fourth item on the agenda of the session, and

Having determined that these proposals shall take the form of a Recommendation supplementing the Discrimination (Employment and Occupation) Convention, 1958;

adopts this twenty-fifth day of June of the year one thousand nine hundred and fifty-eight the following Recommendation, which may be cited as the Discrimination (Employment and Occupation) Recommendation, 1958:

The Conference recommends that each Member should apply the following provisions:

I.   DEFINITIONS

1.   (1) For the purpose of this Recommendation the term "discrimination" includes —

(a) any distinction, exclusion or preference made on the basis of race, colour, sex, religion, political opinion, national extraction or social origin, which has the effect of nullifying or impairing equality of opportunity or treatment in employment or occupation;

(b) such other distinction, exclusion or preference which has the effect of nullifying or impairing equality of opportunity or treatment in employment or occupation as may be determined by the Member concerned after consultation with representative employers' and workers' organisations, where such exist, and with other appropriate bodies.

(2) Any distinction, exclusion or preference in respect of a particular job based on the inherent requirements thereof is not deemed to be discrimination.

(3) For the purpose of this Recommendation the terms "employment" and "occupation" include access to vocational training, access to employment and to particular occupations, and terms and conditions of employment.

II. FORMULATION AND APPLICATION OF POLICY

2. Each Member should formulate a national policy for the prevention of discrimination in employment and occupation. This policy should be applied by means of legislative measures, collective agreements between representative employers' and workers' organisations or in any other manner consistent with national conditions and practice, and should have regard to the following principles:

(a) the promotion of equality of opportunity and treatment in employment and occupation is a matter of public concern;

(b) all persons should, without discrimination, enjoy equality of opportunity and treatment in respect of —
  (i) access to vocational guidance and placement services;
  (ii) access to training and employment of their own choice on the basis of individual suitability for such training or employment;
  (iii) advancement in accordance with their individual character, experience, ability and diligence;
  (iv) security of tenure of employment;
  (v) remuneration for work of equal value;
  (vi) conditions of work including hours of work, rest periods, annual holidays with pay, occupational safety and occupational health measures, as well as social security measures and welfare facilities and benefits provided in connection with employment;

(c) government agencies should apply non-discriminatory employment policies in all their activities;

(d) employers should not practise or countenance discrimination in engaging or training any person for employment, in advancing or retaining such person in employment, or in fixing terms and conditions of employment; nor should any person or organisation obstruct or interfere, either directly or indirectly, with employers in pursuing this principle;

(e) in collective negotiations and industrial relations the parties should respect the principle of equality of opportunity and treatment in employment and occupation, and should ensure that collective agreements contain no provisions of a discriminatory character in respect of access to, training for, advancement in or retention of employment or in respect of the terms and conditions of employment;

(f) employers' and workers' organisations should not practise or countenance discrimination in respect of admission, retention of membership or participation in their affairs.

3. Each Member should —

(a) ensure application of the principles of non-discrimination —

    (i) in respect of employment under the direct control of a national authority;

    (ii) in the activities of vocational guidance, vocational training and placement services under the direction of a national authority;

(b) promote their observance, where practicable and necessary, in respect of other employment and other vocational guidance, vocational training and placement services by such methods as —

    (i) encouraging state, provincial or local government departments or agencies and industries and undertakings operated under public ownership or control to ensure the application of the principles;

    (ii) making eligibility for contracts involving the expenditure of public funds dependent on observance of the principles;

    (iii) making eligibility for grants to training establishments and for a licence to operate a private employment agency or a private vocational guidance office dependent on observance of the principles.

4. Appropriate agencies, to be assisted where practicable by advisory committees composed of representatives of employers' and workers' organisations, where such exist, and of other interested bodies, should be established for the purpose of promoting application of the policy in all fields of public and private employment, and in particular —

(a) to take all practicable measures to foster public understanding and acceptance of the principles of non-discrimination;

(b) to receive, examine and investigate complaints that the policy is not being observed and, if necessary by conciliation, to secure the correction of any practices regarded as in conflict with the policy; and

(c) to consider further any complaints which cannot be effectively settled by conciliation and to render opinions or issue decisions concerning the manner in which discriminatory practices revealed should be corrected.

5. Each Member should repeal any statutory provisions and modify any administrative instructions or practices which are inconsistent with the policy.

6. Application of the policy should not adversely affect special measures designed to meet the particular requirements of persons who, for reasons such as sex, age, disablement, family responsibilities or social or cultural status are generally recognised to require special protection or assistance.

7. Any measures affecting an individual who is justifiably suspected of, or engaged in, activities prejudicial to the security of the State should not be deemed to be discrimination, provided that the individual concerned has the right to appeal to a competent body established in accordance with national practice.

8. With respect to immigrant workers of foreign nationality and the members of their families, regard should be had to the provisions of the Migration for Employment Convention (Revised), 1949, relating to equality of treatment and the provisions of the Migration for Employment Recommendation (Revised), 1949, relating to the lifting of restrictions on access to employment.

9. There should be continuing co-operation between the competent authorities, representatives of employers and workers and appropriate bodies to consider what further positive measures may be necessary in the light of national conditions to put the principles of non-discrimination into effect.

III. CO-ORDINATION OF MEASURES FOR THE PREVENTION OF DISCRIMINATION IN ALL FIELDS

10. The authorities responsible for action against discrimination in employment and occupation should co-operate closely and continuously with the authorities responsible for action against discrimination in other fields in order that measures taken in all fields may be co-ordinated.

STATEMENT FROM THE CONSULTATION ON AIDS AND THE WORKPLACE
(Geneva, 27-29 June 1988)

(World Health Organization in association with International Labour Office)

Three themes were addressed by the Consultation:

* Risk factors associated with HIV infection in the workplace;
* Responses by business and workers to HIV/AIDS; and
* Use of the workplace for health education activities.

The Consultation developed the following consensus statement:

I. General statement

Infection with the human immunodeficiency virus (HIV) and the acquired immunodeficiency syndrome (AIDS) represents an urgent worldwide problem with broad social, cultural, economic, political, ethical and legal dimensions and impact.

National and international AIDS prevention and control efforts have called upon the entire range of health and social services. In this process, in many countries, HIV/AIDS prevention and control problems and efforts have highlighted the weaknesses, inequities and imbalances in existing health and social systems. Therefore, in combating AIDS, an opportunity exists to re-examine and evaluate existing systems as well as assumptions and relationships.

Today there are 2.3 billion economically active people in the world. The workplace plays a central role in the lives of people everywhere. A consideration of HIV/AIDS and the workplace will strengthen the capacity to deal effectively with the problem of HIV/AIDS at the local, national and international levels.

In addition, concern about the spread of HIV/AIDS provides an opportunity to re-examine the workplace environment. It provides workers, employers and their organizations and, where appropriate, governmental agencies and other organizations, with an opportunity to create an atmosphere conducive to caring for and promoting the health of all workers. This may involve a range of issues and concerns, not only individual behaviour, but also addresses matters of collective responsibility. It provides an opportunity to re-examine working relationships in a way that promotes human rights and dignity, ensures freedom from discrimination and stigmatization, and improves working practices and procedures.

II. Introduction

Epidemiological studies from throughout the world have demonstrated that the human immunodeficiency virus (HIV) is transmitted in only three ways:

(a) through sexual intercourse (including semen donation);

(b) through blood (principally blood transfusions and non-sterile injection equipment; also includes organ or tissue transplant);

(c) from infected mother to infant (perinatal transmission).

There is no evidence to suggest the HIV transmission involves insects, food, water, sneezing coughing, toilets, urine, swimming pools, sweat, tears, shared eating and drinking utensils or other items such as protective clothing or telephones. There is no evidence to suggest that HIV can be transmitted by casual, person-to-person contact in any setting.

HIV infection and AIDS (HIV/AIDS) are global problems. At any point in time, the majority of HIV-infected persons are healthy; over time, they may develop AIDS or other HIV-related conditions or they may remain healthy. It is estimated that approximately 90 per cent of the 5-10 million HIV-infected persons worldwide are in the economically productive age group. Therefore, it is natural that questions are asked about the implications of HIV/AIDS for the workplace.

In the vast majority of occupations and occupational settings, work does not involve a risk of acquiring or transmitting HIV between workers, from worker to client, or from client to worker. This document deals with workers who are employed in these occupations. Another consultation to be organized by the WHO Global Programme on AIDS will consider those occupations or occupational situations, such as health workers, in which a recognized risk of acquiring or transmitting HIV may occur.

The purpose of this document is to provide guidance for those considering issues raised by HIV/AIDS and the workplace. Such consideration may involve review of existing health policies or development of new ones.

This document focuses upon the basic principles and core components of policies regarding HIV/AIDS and the workplace.

By addressing the issues raised by HIV/AIDS and the workplace, workers, employers and governments will be able to contribute actively to local, national and international efforts to prevent and control AIDS, in accordance with WHO's Global AIDS Strategy.

III. Policy principles

Protection of the human rights and dignity of HIV-infected persons, including persons with AIDS, is essential to the prevention and control of HIV/AIDS. Workers with HIV infection who are healthy should be treated the same as any other worker. Workers with HIV-related illness, including AIDS, should be treated the same as any other worker with an illness.

Most people with HIV/AIDS want to continue working, which enhances their physical and mental well-being and they should be entitled to do so. They should be enabled to contribute their creativity and productivity in a supportive occupational sitting.

The World Health Assembly resolution (WHA41.24) entitled, "Avoidance of discrimination in relation to HIV-infected people and people with AIDS" urges Member States:

...

(1) to foster a spirit of understanding and compassion for HIV-infected people and people with AIDS ...;

(2) to protect the human rights and dignity of HIV-infected people and people with AIDS ... and to avoid discriminatory action against, and stigmatization of them in the provision of services, employment and travel;

(3) to ensure the confidentiality of HIV testing and to promote the availability of confidential counselling and other support services ...

The approach taken to HIV/AIDS and the workplace must take into account the existing social and legal context, as well as national health policies and the Global AIDS Strategy.

IV. Policy development and implementation

Consistent policies and procedures should be developed at national and enterprise levels through consultations between workers, employers and their organizations, and where appropriate, governmental agencies and other organizations. It is recommended that such policies be developed and implemented before HIV-related questions arise in the workplace.

Policy development and implementation is a dynamic process, not a static event. Therefore, HIV/AIDS workplace policies should be:

(a) communicated to all concerned;

(b) continually reviewed in the light of epidemiological and other scientific information;

(c) monitored for their successful implementation;

(d) evaluated for their effectiveness.

V. Policy components

A. Persons applying for employment

Pre-employment HIV/AIDS screening as part of the assessment of fitness to work is unnecessary and should not be required. Screening of this kind refers to direct methods (HIV testing) or indirect methods (assessment of risk behaviours) or to questions about HIV tests already taken. Pre-employment HIV/AIDS screening for insurance or other purposes raises serious concerns about discrimination and merits close and further scrutiny.

B. Persons in employment

1. **HIV/AIDS screening**. HIV/AIDS screening, whether direct (HIV testing), indirect (assessment of risk behaviours) or asking questions about tests already taken, should not be required.

2. **Confidentiality**. Confidentiality regarding all medical information, including HIV/AIDS status, must be maintained.

3. **Informing the employer**. There should be no obligation of the employee to inform the employer regarding his or her HIV/AIDS status.

4. **Protection of employee**. Persons in the workplace affected by, or perceived to be affected by, HIV/AIDS must be protected from stigmatization and discrimination by co-workers, unions, employers or clients. Information and education are essential to maintain the climate of mutual understanding necessary to ensure this protection.

5. **Access to services for employees**. Employees and their families should have access to information and educational programmes on HIV/AIDS, as well as to relevant counselling and appropriate referral.

6. **Benefits**. HIV-infected employees should not be discriminated against including access to and receipt of benefits from statutory social security programmes and occupationally related schemes.

7. **Reasonable changes in working arrangements**. HIV infection by itself is not associated with any limitation in fitness to work. If fitness to work

is impaired by HIV-related illness, reasonable alternative working arrangements should be made.

8. **Continuation of employment relationship.** HIV infection is not a cause for termination of employment. As with many other illnesses, persons with HIV-related illnesses should be able to work as long as medically fit for available, appropriate work.

9. **First aid.** In any situation requiring first aid in the workplace, precautions need to be taken to reduce the risk of transmitting blood-borne infections, including hepatitis B. These standard precautions will be equally effective against HIV transmission.

ANNEX III

GUIDELINES ON HIV/AIDS AND HUMAN RIGHTS AS ADOPTED BY THE SECOND INTERNATIONAL CONSULTATION ON HIV/AIDS AND HUMAN RIGHTS

(extract of United Nations document E/CN-4/1997/37, adopted by the Commission on Human Rights at its 53rd Session, 20 January 1997)

Guideline 1. States should establish an effective national framework for their response to HIV/AIDS which ensures a coordinated, participatory, transparent and accountable approach, integrating HIV/AIDS policy and programme responsibilities across all branches of Government.

Guideline 2. States should ensure, through political and financial support, that community consultation occurs in all phases of HIV/AIDS policy design, programme implementation and evaluation and that community organizations are enabled to carry out their activities, including in the field of ethics, law and human rights, effectively.

Guideline 3. States should review and reform public health laws to ensure that they adequately address public health issues raised by HIV/AIDS, that their provisions applicable to casually transmitted diseases are not inappropriately applied to HIV/AIDS and that they are consistent with international human rights obligations.

Guideline 4. States should review and reform criminal laws and correctional systems to ensure that they are consistent with international human rights obligations and are not misused in the context of HIV/AIDS or targeted against vulnerable groups.

Guideline 5. States should enact or strengthen anti-discrimination and other protective laws that protect vulnerable groups, people living with HIV/AIDS and people with disabilities from discrimination in both the public and private sectors, ensure privacy and confidentiality and ethics in research involving human subjects, emphasize education and conciliation, and provide for speedy and effective administrative and civil remedies.

Guideline 6. States should enact legislation to provide for the regulation of HIV-related goods, services and information, so as to ensure widespread availability of qualitative preventive measures and services, adequate HIV prevention and care information and safe and effective medication at an affordable price.

Guideline 7. States should implement and support legal support services that will educate people affected by HIV/AIDS about their rights, provide free legal services to enforce these rights, develop expertise on HIV-related legal issues and utilize means of protection in addition to the courts, such as offices of ministries of justice, ombudspersons, health complaint units and human rights commissions.

Guideline 8. States, in collaboration with and through the community, should promote a supportive and enabling environment for women, children and other vulnerable groups by addressing underlying prejudices and inequalities through community dialogue, specially designed social and health services and support to community groups.

Guideline 9. States should promote the wide and ongoing distribution of creative education, training and media programmes explicitly designed to change attitudes of discrimination and stigmatization associated with HIV/AIDS to understanding and acceptance.

Guideline 10. States should ensure that government and private sectors develop codes of conduct regarding HIV/AIDS issues that translate human rights principles into codes of professional responsibility and practice, with accompanying mechanisms to implement and enforce these codes.

Guideline 11. States should ensure monitoring and enforcement mechanisms to guarantee the protection of HIV-related human rights, including those of people living with HIV/AIDS, their families and communities.

Guideline 12. States should cooperate through all relevant programmes and agencies of the United Nations system, including UNAIDS, to share knowledge and experience concerning HIV-related human rights issues and should ensure effective mechanisms to protect human rights in the context of HIV/AIDS at international level.

AIDS AGREEMENT BETWEEN THE NATIONAL UNION OF MINEWORKERS AND THE CHAMBER OF MINES OF SOUTH AFRICA

Concluded between the parties as provided for in the agreement of 31 July 1991, concerning the 1991 review of wages and other conditions of employment

Objective

The objective of this agreement is to provide industry-level guidelines:

(a) to minimize the effect of HIV in the mining industry;

(b) to prevent the spread of HIV infection; and

(c) for the management of HIV infection in the employer/employee relationship.

Policy

1. General principle

Whilst recognizing that there are circumstances unique to HIV infection, the fundamental principle to be applied is that HIV infection and AIDS should be approached on the same basis as any other serious condition.

2. Rights of the individual employee

2.1 *Rights of employees who are HIV-positive*

HIV-positive employees will be protected against discrimination, victimization or harassment.

2.2 *Testing*

No employee should be required to undergo an HIV test at the request, or upon the initiative of management or an employee organization, provided that where HIV testing is intended in specified occupations on medical grounds, the employee will be required to undergo testing where this has been supported by the independent and objective medical assessment of a medical practitioner, mutually agreed to by the parties. Failing agreement the Medical Bureau for Occupational Diseases will be requested to select such a practitioner.

2.3 Employment opportunities and termination of employment

No employee should suffer adverse consequences, whether dismissal or denial or appropriate alternative employment opportunities which exist, merely on the basis of HIV infection.

2.4 Counselling

Appropriate support and counselling services will be made available to employees.

2.5 Benefits

Employees who are clinically ill or medically unfit for work will enjoy benefits in terms of the relevant conditions of employment as negotiated from time to time between the parties.

3. Epidemiological testing

3.1 Testing programmes for epidemiological purposes will be the subject of appropriate consultation with recognized employee organizations, and will be subject to independent and objective evaluation and scrutiny.

3.2 The statistical results of testing programmes will be shared with employees and recognized employee organizations.

3.3 The results of epidemiological studies will not be used as a basis for discriminating against any class of employee in the workplace.

4. Testing standards

4.1 All testing will comply with generally accepted international standards (on pre- and post-test counselling, informed consent, confidentiality and support).

5. Awareness and education programmes

5.1 In the absence of vaccine or cure, information and education are vital components of an AIDS prevention programme because the spread of the disease can be limited by informed and responsible behaviour.

5.2 Appropriate awareness and education programmes will be conducted to inform employees about AIDS and HIV which will enable them to protect themselves and others against infection by HIV.

5.3 The involvement of employees and their recognized representatives is of key importance in awareness, education and counselling programmes to prevent the spread of AIDS as well as in the support for HIV-positive employees.

5.4 The employers will consult with employees and their recognized representatives on current and future programmes (referred to in clause 5.3) and their implementation, at mine level.

6. Lifestyle changes

6.1 It is acknowledged that it is the role of each individual to prevent the transmission of HIV through informed and responsible behaviour and the parties also recognize that socio-economic circumstances can influence disease patterns in communities.

6.2 The parties agree to consider at mine level the socio-economic environment and lifestyles in relation to the effective prevention of HIV infection.

7. Health care workers

7.1 The policy recognizes the professional and ethical guidelines for health care workers as stipulated by the relevant statutory bodies.

8. Joint discussions

8.1 The signatory employee organizations undertake to participate in joint meetings with other interested parties, where necessary, to give effect to the terms of this agreement.

9. Amendment to agreement

9.1 The parties jointly undertake to assess and review the efficacy of the provisions of this policy one year after its implementation, or at any stage thereafter.

Signed by the National Union of Mineworkers and the Chamber of Mines on behalf of recognizing mines at Johannesburg on this 25th day of August 1993.